Let's Listen

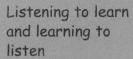

Listening to learn
and learning to
listen

Written by Clare Beswick and Sally Featherstone

Illustrated by Martha Hardy

A *Little* Baby Book
Published by Featherstone Education

**Heads up lookers
and communicators**

**Sitters, standers
and explorers**

**Movers, shakers
and players**

**Walkers, talkers
and pretenders**

About Little Baby Books

'Birth to Three Matters' (DfES SureStart 2002), the framework for effective practice with babies and very young children, sends a clear unequivocal message underlining the importance of home and family working together with practitioners to lay the best possible foundations for life and learning. It is a recognition and celebration of the individuality of babies and young children. It provides a wealth of guidance and support to those with responsibility for their care and education.

The Little Baby Book series builds on the principles of the guidance and provides practical handbooks, with a wealth of easy to follow ideas and activities for babies and young children from birth to three.

All the activities use objects and resources readily available in homes and settings. They allow babies and children to develop at their own pace, to make unhurried discoveries and allow for much repetition as well as trying out of new ideas. They encourage children to become increasingly independent, making their own choices. All the activities require the careful and skilful support of an adult. The role of the adult is included in the step-by-step 'What you do' section.

The Birth to Three framework identifies four aspects which highlight the skills and competence of babies and young children as well as showing the link between growth, learning, development and the environment in which they are cared for and educated.

These four aspects of the framework are:
A strong child (Purple Books)   **A skilful communicator** (Pink Books)
A competent learner (Green Books)   **A healthy child** (Blue Books)

About 'Let's Listen'

Let's Listen is part of the Little Baby Books series and focuses on the aspect –
A Skilful Communicator.

Within this aspect there are two components:
* listening and responding (gaining attention, developing listening skills)
* making meaning (looking, pointing,naming, making sounds and words)

The process of becoming a skilful communicator starts at birth and needs ongoing and indefinite refinement, development and practice. Communication is fundamental to learning and socialising. It is the bedrock of our ability to function in the world and to relate to each other, explore, learn and create.

Every baby and young child develops at their own rate and, in a stimulating and responsive environment, they progress from stage to stage spontaneously. However, there is much that early years practitioners and parents can do to tune into babies' and young children's communication, support their development of language and share their joy and wonder as they move towards becoming skilful and effective communicators.

Aspect:
A Skilful Communicator
Component:
listening and responding

3

Let's
Listen

Listening to learn
and learning to
listen

The focus of 'Let's Listen'

Let's Listen, part of the Little Baby Book series, focuses on the aspect *a skilful communicator*. Within this aspect there are four components:

* Being together   * Finding a voice
* Listening and responding   * Making meaning

Listening and responding is the focus of this Little Baby Book. It is about babies and young children discovering the joy and flow of effective communication. They learn about imitating others, using sounds and actions, as well as using and understanding a wealth of non verbal signals and clues.

All the activities in this book aim to enable babies and young children to:

* become confident.   * develop trust.
* make choices.   * develop awareness of own needs.
* become aware of needs of others.   * practice early interaction skills.
* take turns.   * develop language skills.
* have a sense of shared fun.   * develop listening skills.
* imitate actions.   * practice being attentive.
* develop simple pretend play.   * explore and discover.
* develop a sense of curiosity. * encounter genuine praise.

Your role as practitioner or parent will be varied and will include:

* Facilitating   * Observing   * Prompting   * Negotiating
* Leading   * Imitating   * Focusing

Each activity page has numerous ideas and suggestions. These include tips and advice on supporting children with special needs, and plenty of 'Ready for more' ideas for children who are ready for the next stage.

Watch, listen, reflect

Assessing babies' and children's learning is a difficult process, but we do know that any assessment must be based on careful observation of children in action.

On each activity page, you will see a box labelled **Watch, listen, reflect**. This box contains suggestions of what you might look and listen for as you work and play with the babies and children. Much of the time you will watch, listen and <u>remember</u>, using your knowledge of early years and of the children and reflecting on the progress of the individual child. These informal observations will help you to plan the next day's or week's activities.

However, sometimes what you see is new evidence - something you have never seen the child do before, or something which concerns you. In these cases you might make a written note of what you see, and the date and time you observed it. You will use these notes for a range of different purposes, and some of these are:

- 👁 to remind you of the event or achievement (it's easy to forget in a busy setting!).
- 👁 to use in discussion with your manager or other practitioners.
- 👁 to contribute to the child's profile or record.
- 👁 to discuss with parents.
- 👁 to help with identifying or supporting additional needs.
- 👁 to help with planning for individuals.
- 👁 to make sure you tell everyone about the child's achievements.

Observation is a crucial part of the complex job you do, and time spent observing and listening to children is never wasted.

Keeping safe

Listening to learn
and learning to
listen

Safety must be the top priority when working with any baby or young child, at nursery or at home. All the activities in Little Baby Books are suitable for under threes. You will already have a health and safety policy but here are just a few top tips for safe playing with babies and young children.

Watch for choking hazards

Young babies and children naturally explore toys by bringing them to their mouths. This is fine, but always check that toys are clean. If you are concerned, buy a choke measure from a high street baby shop.

Never leave babies or young children unattended

They are naturally inquisitive and this needs to be encouraged, BUT they need you to watch out for them. Make sure you are always there.

Check for sharp edges

Some everyday objects or wooden toys can splinter. Check all toys and equipment regularly. Don't leave this to chance – make a rota.

Ribbons and string

Mobiles and toys tied to baby gyms are a great way to encourage looking and reaching, but do check regularly that they are fastened securely. Ribbons and string are fascinating for babies and children of all ages but they can be a choking hazard.

Clean spaces

Babies are natural explorers. They need clean floors. Store outdoor shoes away from the under threes area.

Sitters and standers

Make sure of a soft landing for babies and young children just getting there with sitting and standing balance. Put a pillow behind babies who are just starting to sit. Keep the area clear of hard objects, such as wooden bricks. Look out for trip hazards for crawlers and walkers.

High and low chairs

Make sure babies and young children are fastened securely into high chairs and that chairs are moved out of the way when not in use. Use a low chair and table for young children. Try a foot-rest if their feet don't reach the ground. Watch out for chairs that tip easily.

Contents

Let's Listen

Listening to learn and learning to listen

Aspect:
A Skilful Communicator
Component:
listening and responding

Listening to learn
and learning to
listen

**Heads up lookers
and communicators**

Aspect:
A Skilful
Communicator
Component:
Listening and
responding

8

Copy cat! -
copying facial expressions

What you need

* a few moments of one to one
  quiet time
* a comfortable place to sit
  with the baby

What you do

1. Hold the baby, with head well supported so that you can
   gaze into the baby's face with ease.
2. Remember that young babies focus best around 20 to 35
   cm. that is 8 to 15 inches. Make sure you are close
   enough for the baby to be able to see you clearly.
3. Sing hello to the baby. Stroke cheeks and gently engage
   the baby's attention. Pause and then stick your tongue
   out! Repeat this every 20 seconds or so. Keep going for
   about two minutes to give the baby plenty of time to
   respond by copying your action.

another idea:
* Try some different actions, such as wriggling your nose,
  smiling and so on. Repeat the action for one to two minutes
  allowing the baby plenty of time to copy your actions.

Ready for more?

🖐 Use a baby mirror
   together, gazing at
   your baby's reflection.
🖐 Play anticipation
   games, such as 'I'm
   coming to tickle you'.
🖐 Sing rhymes and songs,
   patting the rhythm out
   on their tummy or back.

Individual needs

☼ Support the baby's head well until full head control is achieved.

☼ Strongly contrasting colours and patterns are best for young children at an early developmental stage.

☼ Allow plenty of time for responses. Prompting while they are thinking may throw them off course!

Tiny Tip

❋ Makethe movements slowly and give plenty of time for the baby to respond.

Watch, listen, reflect

👁 Look to see how the baby is focusing and following your eyes.

👁 Think about how they are showing their feelings. Are they pleased when they succeed in copying you?

👁 Think about head control and sitting balance for older babies. Does this affect how they respond to you?

👁 Listen to the sounds the baby is making. How do they respond?

Working together

Parents could:

* fix a small baby mirror to their child's baby gym or mobile.
* try some 'Ready steady go' play with their baby.

Practitioners could:

* make a booklet of finger rhymes and action songs you use for parents to borrow for home.
* make sure parents know that young babies focus best at 20 to 35 cm., 8 to 15 inches, and what this means for playing, singing and talking.

Let's Listen

Listening to learn and learning to listen

What are they learning?

are they
　looking?
　listening?
　responding?
　copying actions?
　interacting?
this leads to
　* attention and listening skills
　* understanding
　* turn taking

9

Heads up lookers and communicators

Aspect:
A Skilful Communicator

Component:
Listening and responding

10

Fingers and toes –
finger puppet fun

What you need

* some bright green fur fabric
* fabric glue or a simple sewing kit
* scissors

What you do

1. Make a very simple green caterpillar finger puppet to fit your index finger. Use fabric glue or simple stitches to fix the sides.
2. Have the baby well supported, so that you can gaze into each other's eyes, perhaps sitting sideways on your knee.
3. Try this new finger rhyme, gradually wriggling and creeping the finger puppet up the baby's arm into the palm of their hand, round and round and then down their arm, tummy, legs to their toes.

   Wriggle, wriggle, here I come, caterpillar on my thumb
   Round and round, off he goes, all the way down to my toes

another idea:

* Start the rhyme very slowly and pause before running your fingers down to the baby's toes for a gentle tickle.

Ready for more?

✋ Put the baby's hands between your own and rub them gently, singing 'Rub a dub dub, rub a dub dub'.
✋ Lie the baby on their back, hold their ankles in the air, and play 'peek a boo' between their feet.

Individual needs

☼ Some children may prefer a gentle pressure to a very light touch.

☼ Gently rub your fingers across the back of fisted hands to help the child to relax muscles and open their hand.

☼ Stopping in the middle of a rhyme, with an exaggerated pause and gasp is a great attention grabber.

Tiny Tip

❋ Inviting people to make simple finger puppets is a good way to get the others involved in your setting.

Watch, listen, reflect

👁 Watch to see if the baby is anticipating the tickle.

👁 See how the baby lets you know they want the activity repeated.

👁 Think about how they are using sounds, body language, expression and eye contact to ask for more.

👁 Listen to the sounds they are making, and note the timing of them.

Working together

Parents could:

* try some finger puppet fun at home.
* borrow some rhyme and action songs books from the local library.

Practitioners could:

* tell parents which are their baby's favourite songs, within the group.
* talk with parents about the range of ways their baby is making their needs and preferences known.

Let's Listen

Listening to learn and learning to listen

What are they learning?

are they
looking?
anticipating?
attending?
sharing attention?
this leads to
* attention and listening skills
* understanding
* babbling and first words

11

Heads up lookers and communicators

Aspect:
A Skilful Communicator

Component:
Listening and responding

Baby dance –
moving to a rhythm together

What you need

* an adult with each baby
* a warm, comfortable familiar place

  <u>Remember</u> - this is a game for babies with good head control.

What you do

1. Make a circle with each adult standing and holding the baby under their arms, with the babies facing the adults.
2. Move around the circle taking steady side steps and sing together, using a tune you are comfortable with:

   Step and step, 1, 2, 3, step and step, dance with me,
   Step and step, 1, 2, 3, step and stop and look at me!

   On the last line, stop suddenly, swing the babies gently high in the air, hold them there, hold their eye contact for a moment before swinging them gently down again and continuing the dance.

another idea:

* Try this game with the babies facing away from the adults. They will love watching each other.

Ready for more?

🖐 Sit in a circle with an adult supporting each baby on the floor. Pat a large beach ball around the circle.

🖐 Still in the circle, give each baby a large floppy hat. Play a game of tipping the hats off.

Individual needs

- Make sure the babies have good head control and enjoy this sort of game.
- Play each game with one adult and baby to help confidence and reassurance. Later, bring just one more well-settled baby into the game.
- Quicken the pace and make the game livelier for older babies.

Tiny Tip

An exaggerated gasp is a winner when trying to grab the attention of babies and young children.

Watch, listen, reflect

- Watch to see if the babies are anticipating the lift in the air.
- See if they seek to engage your eye contact and attention when you lift them high in the air.
- Are they comfortable moving with you to the rhythm of the dance?
- Listen to the range of sounds they use to tell you they like the game.

Working together

Parents could:

* dance and sing together. Babies and children love to share adults' music.
* tell practitioners what sort of music their baby likes at home.

Practitioners could:

* build up a collection of varied music to enjoy with the babies.
* make dancing and enjoying music together a small part of every day.

Let's Listen

Listening to learn and learning to listen

What are they learning?

are they
moving together?
feeling rhythm?
sharing fun?
showing trust?
anticipating?
this leads to
* shared attention
* focusing
* repetition and imitation

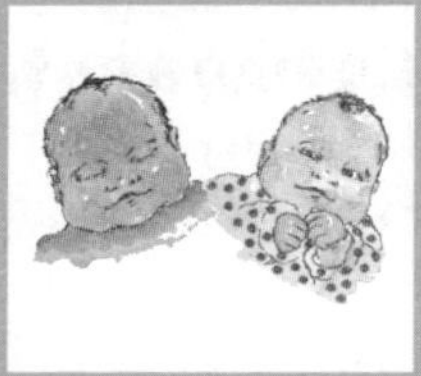

Sitters, standers and explorers

Aspect:
A Skilful Communicator

Component:
Listening and responding

Oops, my hat! -
practising 'Give me' gestures

What you need

* several large floppy silly hats
* a baby-safe mirror

What you do

1. Explore the hats together. Put the hats on and play at tipping or pulling them off.
2. Next put all the hats away except one. Give this hat to the child and ask them to put it on your head. Prompt them with natural gestures and single words.
3. Say 'Ready steady go' and then shake your head vigorously so the hat falls off! When the child retrieves the hat, use an outstretched hand and words to ask them to hand you the hat. Play again, this time putting the hat on the child's head. Show them their reflection, before doing 'Ready steady go' to start them pulling or tipping the hat off!

another idea:

* Play again, encouraging the children to put hats on each other's heads and return them to your 'give me' hand gesture.

Ready for more?

- Play this game with large plastic bangles, putting them on and then shaking them off.
- Share a simple inset board together, asking the child to take out and pass you each piece of the puzzle.

14

Individual needs

- Play one to one with young babies and children who need particular help with early attention and social skills.
- Make sure there is a soft landing for babies and toddlers who tip over as they reach for things.
- Use pointing and natural gesture to support understanding.

Tiny Tip

Pointing is a real milestone on the way to becoming an effective communicator.

Watch, listen, reflect

- Watch the body language and facial expression, that the children are using to support their moves towards spoken language.
- Look for pointing to make requests, as well as pointing to show you things of interest.
- Watch to see how children grasp the idea of the game on repetition and how they anticipate their turn.

Working together

Parents could:

* collect together a few clothes for some dressing up fun.
* talk to practitioners about the sort of games, play and times when their baby is most vocal, and the sorts of sounds and babble they hear.

Practitioners could:

* make sure a baby safe wall mirror is fixed at the right height for babies and young children to look in. Put an appropriate handle or steady bit of furniture close by for older babies to pull up and see themselves standing.

Listening to learn and learning to listen

What are they learning?

are they
- anticipating?
- understanding natural gesture?
- taking turns?
- pointing?

this leads to
- * first words
- * being in a group
- * following simple rules and routines

Let's Listen

Listening to learn and learning to listen

Sitters, standers and explorers

Aspect:
A Skilful Communicator

Component:
Listening and responding

What's that? –
exploring everyday objects

What you need
* a collection of small boxes and bags
* several everyday objects such as cup, spoon, flannel, brush, shoe, sock etc.

What you do
1. Place two or three everyday objects in each box and bag.
2. Play together exploring the boxes and bags. Name each object but also talk about how it feels, looks and also what it is used for. Use simple single words and two or three word phrases. Use lots of natural gesture.
3. Demonstrate the use of the object, such as pretending to brush your hair with the brush and so on. Invite the children to copy your actions.
4. Allow plenty of time for unhurried, uninterrupted exploration.

another idea:
* Play again, choosing a range of familiar objects from home, but those less frequently used by the child, such as a key, pen, gloves, nailbrush, egg cup, whisk and so on.

Ready for more?
☝ Use two of each object and hunt for pairs.
☝ Play with a small cupboard of everyday objects, filling, emptying, opening and closing.
☝ Try everyday objects in a very shallow tray of bubbly water.

Individual needs

☼ With children at an early developmental stage, start with just two or three objects of particular interest to them.

☼ Help children develop understanding or routines, by giving them an object such as a spoon to hold, just before dinner, or perhaps their coat to feel, just before going out.

Tiny Tip

❈ Talk with colleagues about the value of pointing and natural gesture in the setting to ensure it is used consistently.

Watch, listen, reflect

👁 Look for children spontaneously demonstrating an object's use.

👁 Watch to see if children can imitate actions.

👁 Listen for attempts at first words, and the sounds being used.

👁 Think about the range of ways the children are communicating with you and with the other children.

Working together

Parents could:

* set aside a cupboard or box that children can empty and refill.
* let their child hold and explore safe everyday objects and join in imitating simple house-hold tasks.
* bring things from home to use in the game.

Practitioners could:

* find out from parents what sort of toys and resources are most appealing to the child and how they use them.
* tell parents how their child's understanding of language is growing and what is done in the setting to support this.

Let's Listen

Listening to learn and learning to listen

What are they learning?

are they
   using objects?
   understanding gesture?
   pointing?
   using first words?
this leads to
   * first words
   * simple pretend play
   * listening skills

17

Let's
Listen

Listening to learn
and learning to
listen

**Sitters, standers
and explorers**

Aspect:
A Skilful
Communicator
Component:
Listening and
responding

Look, over there! -
touch and distance pointing

What you need
* shoes, hat, socks, gloves
* a large doll

What you do

1. Play at dressing and undressing the doll together, talking about each item of clothing, and asking the child to show you where each item goes. Encourage them to touch-point to different body parts on the doll, such as 'Look, it's a hat, where does this go?' pause, 'On dolly's head'.
2. Now take one of the items, and ask a child to put it 'over there', pointing to a chair or table a metre or so away. Encourage the child to look where you are pointing and help you put the item of clothing there. Continue until the hat, shoes, gloves and socks are all about one metre away, but in different directions.
4. Help the child to find each item. Ask 'Where are the gloves?' distance point to the gloves and say, 'Gloves, let's put them on dolly'. Continue to use pointing.

Ready for more?

🖐 Use a pointing gesture to make choices, such as between two different cups or snacks at drink time.
🖐 Practice isolating index fingers by pressing and squashing single Rice Krispies or cornflakes.

Individual needs

☼ Most children with autistic spectrum disorders find pointing to make a request or share some information with another person very difficult, but pointing can be an invaluable tool for children with communication difficulties, so it needs to be encouraged.

Tiny Tip

✳ Pointing can mean 'what's that?' 'I want', 'give me', 'it's that one', or 'look at that'. Always use words as well to help language development.

Watch, listen, reflect

👁 Watch to see if children are spontaneously pointing to named objects or body parts.

👁 Think about the way they are using, and how they understand a touch point and a distance point.

👁 Look for emerging understanding of body part words on their own body, *name's* nose, your nose and dolly's nose.

Working together

Parents could:

* use natural gesture and pointing as they talk to their child.
* point out distance objects, such as aeroplanes overhead, birds in trees and so on.

Practitioners could:

* ask parents how their child uses pointing and natural gesture at home.
* talk about the different ways pointing and gesture are used in everyday routines within the setting.

Let's Listen

Listening to learn and learning to listen

What are they learning?

are they
  using gesture?
  using pointing?
  naming body parts?
  using words and gestures?
this leads to
  * understanding words and phrases
  * listening

Listening to learn and learning to listen

Sitters, standers and explorers

Aspect:
A Skilful Communicator
Component:
Listening and responding

'Up,' and 'All gone' -
using natural gesture

What you need

* basket of ball-pool balls, or similar light balls

What you do

1. Tip the balls out of the basket together. Say and gesture (both hands raised palms upwards) 'All gone!'
2. Help the children to put the balls back in the basket. Stand up with the basket and with all of you holding the basket, lift it as high in the air as the children can reach. Encourage them to let go, and then keep lifting the basket in the air, and then pause and ask ' Up?' Encourage the children to raise both arms in the air, in an 'Up' gesture. Move the basket a little higher...
3. Say 'Ready, steady go' and throw the balls up into the air from the basket. Show the children the empty basket, say and gesture 'All gone'. Do it all again, and again, and again!

another idea:
* Use clean craft feathers on a tray or piece of thick card.

Ready for more?

- Play at filling and emptying water or coloured rice from jugs and cups into a tray or plastic box. Use 'All gone', words and gestures.
- Get children to raise their arms and say 'Up' when coming to you for a hug.

20

Individual needs

☼ Children with Down's syndrome often have a visual learning style and find gesture particularly helpful.

☼ Play this game with just two children if children are at an early developmental stage or have physical difficulties.

☼ Rolled up socks make 'easy-to-hold' balls.

Tiny Tip

✳ Get together with other staff and make sure you all use the same natural gestures.

Watch, listen, reflect

👁 Watch to see how they imitate the gestures and actions. Are they able to use these gestures spontaneously at other times?

👁 Listen to the sounds and attempts at first words used to support the gestures.

👁 Think about the other natural gestures each child uses.

Working together

Parents could:

✳ use the words and gesture for 'all gone' consistently at mealtimes.

✳ encourage their child to use gestures only in context and with real meaning such as waving 'Bye' when someone is going.

Practitioners could:

✳ use natural gesture with songs and action rhymes.

✳ talk to parents about their child's use of gesture, pointing and sounds.

Let's Listen

Listening to learn and learning to listen

What are they learning?

are they
    understanding 'all gone'?
    using sounds and gesture together?
    sharing fun?
    imitating actions?
this leads to
    * small group play
    * turn taking
    * sharing

Movers, shakers and players

Aspect:
A Skilful Communicator

Component:
Listening and responding

More than one -
finding, matching and first sorting

What you need

* two each of a selection of everyday objects, such as toy cars, books, balls, dustpan and brushes, sponges, bricks, wooden spoons, etc.
* a large cloth

What you do

1. Spread the pairs of everyday objects out on the cloth. Ask each child to choose an object. Now see if you can all find another of the same.
2. Talk about the different objects and pretend to use them. Use action words as well as object words.
3. Next, hide all the objects under the cloth. Lie down around the edge and feel under the cloth to see what objects you can find. Any pairs? Remember, no peeking!

another idea:

* Play this game with lots of cars, bricks and books. See if the children can pull all the cars out from under the cloth, all the books, all the bricks and so on by feel alone.

Ready for more?

- Practice sorting cutlery into a cutlery tray, all the spoons together, all the forks and so on.
- Make a pile of bricks and toy cars. Pull out all the cars to make a traffic jam, and all the bricks to make a tower.

Individual needs

- ✿ Start with just two or three pairs of very familiar everyday objects, such as cup, toy car and shoe, for children at an early developmental stage.
- ✿ Use natural gesture and pointing to provide clues and prompts to help children's emerging understanding of language.

Tiny Tip

- ✳ Sort and store every day objects near where they are used, so children can link objects and use.

Watch, listen, reflect

- 👁 Look to see if children understand the use of the objects, as well as their name labels.
- 👁 Listen for first words, object words as well as action words.
- 👁 Watch to see if children understand the concept of 'same'.
- 👁 Can the children relate the objects used in the activity to other objects they see around them?

Working together

Parents could:

- ∗ help their child to sort and match into pairs a pile of socks.
- ∗ look for photograph books of everyday objects and share these with their child, using object and action words.

Practitioners could:

- ∗ share with parents how first words and early understanding are encouraged in the setting.
- ∗ put up a poster with ideas of what to look for when choosing picture books and storybooks, with details of the local library.

What are they learning?

are they
    using object names?
    finding the same?
    using sounds and gesture together?
this leads to
    * using first words and phrases
    * following simple rules

23

Movers, shakers and players

Aspect:
A Skilful Communicator

Component:
Listening and responding

Clap, clap, stamp, stamp –
imitating actions and sounds

What you need
* a basket of gloves
* some wrist toys

What you do

1. With the gloves and wrist toys out of sight, sit with two or three children on the floor. Using a tune you are comfortable with and actions to accompany the words, sing:
    I have two hands to clap, clap, clap, clap,
    I have two feet to stamp, stamp, stamp, stamp
    Clap, clap, clap, stamp, stamp, stamp
2. Now, let the children choose some gloves, and sing the rhyme and do the actions again with you.
3. Next, offer the children the wrist toys to wear on their ankles! Try the rhyme again.

another idea:
*   Try it with an odd assortment of dressing up footwear, perhaps fluffy slippers, wellington boots, tap shoes or perhaps flippers!

Ready for more?

🖐 Vary the pace of the song. Try it very quickly and then very very slowly.

🖐 Play stamping games outside in puddles, on gravel, on grass on the path.

Individual needs

☼ Match the actions of the song to the physical abilities of children within the group.

☼ Encourage children with fine motor difficulties to bring two hands to the midline.

☼ Keep the game short and lively for children with attention difficulties.

Tiny Tip

✳ Sew small bells securely onto elastic for some quick, easy and effective wrist toys.

Watch, listen, reflect

👁 Watch to see if the children are remembering the rhyme and actions, anticipating the next action.

👁 Watch how they make and express choices of gloves and wrist toys.

👁 Listen to the range of sounds and single words they are using.

👁 Think about how they imitate other actions during the day, perhaps in simple pretend play.

Working together

Parents could:

* try some new action rhymes with their child.
* add a few minutes of rhymes to bedtime routine.

Practitioners could:

* create a book of favourite action rhymes for loan to parents.
* talk to parents about the importance of imitation in early learning, and the sorts of opportunities for imitation offered within the setting.

Let's Listen

Listening to learn and learning to listen

What are they learning?

are they
imitating actions?
using action words?
enjoying being in a small group?
making choices?
this leads to
* listening skills
* joining in with action rhymes

Movers, shakers and players

Aspect:
A Skilful Communicator
Component:
Listening and responding

In it goes -
posting objects and pictures

What you need

* picture-pairs games
* cardboard tubes, such as potato snack tubes
* scissors, glue, red paper and a black marker pen

What you do

1. Cut a posting slot in the tube. Cover the tube with red paper to make a simple posting box. Use the marker pen to add some details and highlight the edge of the posting slot.
2. Choose six different cards, starting with pictures of familiar objects. Spread the cards face down on the floor or table.
3. Take turns with the child to choose a card. Give them time to name the card. If they don't attempt to name it, say for example, 'Name, look, car'. Post the card into the box and say 'Car gone'.
4. Take turns. Talk about the pictures and relate them to objects you can see around you in your setting.

another idea:
* Make a larger post box and post real everyday objects.

Ready for more?

🖐 Turn the cards face up and ask the child to find a card by name, such as 'Where's the flower?' then post it.
🖐 Ask older children to take turns to tell <u>you</u> which card to find.

Individual needs

☼ For children at an early developmental level, use real objects or photographs of real objects.

☼ Use real objects and a bright yellow posting box for children with visual difficulties.

☼ accept different ways of responding.

Tiny Tip

�֍ Give the game a definite end, such as shaking the post box and then tipping all the cards back into the pairs box.

Watch, listen, reflect

👁 Note if they understand single object words. Do they show understanding of the use of the objects?

👁 Listen for attempts at first words, and sounds combined with gestures and pointing.

👁 Consider each child's understanding of language, as well as their expressive language.

Working together

Parents could:

* spend a few minutes every day looking at books and pictures with their child.
* talk about pictures they see as they go out and about together.

Practitioners could:

* make sure that a good range of picture books is available and update these regularly.
* check the picture-pairs and lotto games in the setting to ensure different styles of images, photographs and line drawings are available.

Let's Listen

Listening to learn and learning to listen

What are they learning?

are they understanding first words and simple rules?
listening?
taking turns?
attending?
this leads to
* attention
* taking part in a simple game

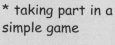

27

Movers, shakers and players

Aspect:
A Skilful Communicator

Component:
Listening and responding

Give me a clue -
understanding daily routines and sequences

What you need

* a camera
* card and a marker pen

What you do

1. Make a list of the main activities and routines within the setting, such as meals, snacks, group time, different play activities, looking at books going outside.
2. Take photographs of each of these activities. Mount these on card and use the marker pen to add simple line drawing borders which add additional clues, such as on the photo of the tray of cups, add a border of milk bottles, water jugs, straws, etc.
3. Show some of the photos to the children. Talk about them and use these photographs to help children know what is happening next, such as showing them the 'Dinner time' photo card, when it is time to get ready.
4. Also, use the cards to help the children make choices about what they want to play with or put outside.

Ready for more?

🖐 Make a visual timetable for older children by fixing the photos to the wall in the order in which they will occur that day. As each activity passes, take that photo down.

28

Individual needs

☼ Use objects rather than photographs as prompts for visually impaired children and those at an early developmental stage.

☼ For children with fine motor difficulties, make sure the photographs are mounted on chunky card, and shaped for easy grip.

Tiny Tip

�֍ Make sure all practitioners in the setting use the child's name first when talking to individuals.

Watch, listen, reflect

👁 Listen for attempts at first words, object and action words to describe the images.

👁 Watch how individual children relate the photographs to activities and routines.

👁 Watch to see how children find details in the pictures. Look for pointing and natural gesture.

Working together

Parents could:

* bring in photos of their child and family for practitioners to share with the child.

* talk to children about what is happening next, giving them clues and reminders to help early understanding.

Practitioners could:

* talk to parents about how understanding of language emerges from everyday objects, experiences and routines.

* develop a poster or fact sheet for parents with ideas of what could be done at home to support language development.

Let's Listen

Listening to learn and learning to listen

What are they learning?

are they
  using object names, first words and phrases?
  using clues and prompts?
  making choices?
  listening?
this leads to
  * sustained attention

Listening to learn
and learning to
listen

**Walkers, talkers
and pretenders**

Aspect:
A Skilful
Communicator
Component:
Listening and
responding

Hands together -
copying actions

What you need

* a quiet space and a clear
  table top

What you do

Work with a small group on this activity.

1. Sit at the table, with two or three children standing
   around the edge, one on each side of the table. You
   should all be more or less at the same level, so it is easy
   to gaze into each other's face and make good eye contact.
2. Place both your hands flat on the table and encourage
   the children to do the same. Use the following rhyme to
   walk your fingers across the table, until you touch the
   fingers of the child opposite, or next to you.
   Walking, walking, off we go (walk fingers across table)
   Walking, walking 'til we meet (walk until you meet)
   Say hello! hello! hello! (lift hands and touch open palms)
   Walking, walking back we go (walk back across the table)
   Continue playing using different directions and actions.

Ready for more?

- Pass a handshake
  around a circle of
  children, first one way
  then the other.
- Play the traditional
  stacking hands game,
  taking turns to put one
  hand on top of the
  other, making a pile.

30

Individual needs

☼ Pat the table rather than walking with fingers for children with fine motor difficulties.

☼ Help children with clenched hands to release to an open hand by gently rubbing the back of their hands.

☼ Children with visual difficulties need to sit in a good, but not glaring, light.

Tiny Tip

❋ Collect purses and bags, add some jewellery and hats for some great dressing up corner fun.

Watch, listen, reflect

◉ Look at how children imitate the actions and are able to link their actions to the words of the song.

◉ Watch to see if children are aware of each other's needs.

◉ Look to see how they are able to maintain their concentration.

◉ Are the children able to separate their fingers and imitate the walking fingers action?

Working together

Parents could:

* try this game at home, perhaps along the edge of the bath at bath time.
* look for books and tapes of finger rhymes at the local library or toy library.

Practitioners could:

* remind parents of the traditional stacking hands game and talk about the importance of this sort of shared fun.
* take turns to learn a new finger rhyme to share with colleagues and children.

Let's Listen

Listening to learn and learning to listen

What are they learning?

are they
   aware of the needs of others?
   part of a group?
   imitating actions?
   respecting other children's personal space?
this leads to
   * attention
   * group work

Listening to learn and learning to listen

Walkers, talkers and pretenders

Aspect:
A Skilful Communicator
Component:
Listening and responding

Dolly, do this –
understanding action words

What you need

For each child:
* a teddy or doll, brush, flannel, blanket and cup
* another set for you!

What you do

Work with a small group on this activity.
1. Sit with the children and join in with this simple pretend play.
2. Focus on using action words and prompting the children to use action words. Comment on what they are doing.
3. Use and prompt two word phrases to describe possession, such as Teddy's cup, or Dolly's face.
4. Build sequences of play, such as giving Teddy a drink, a hug and then covering with a blanket for sleep.

another idea:
* Sing an action rhyme together such as, 'Here we go Round the Mulberry Bush', 'This is the way we brush Teddy's hair, brush Teddy's hair, brush Teddy's hair, this is the way we brush Teddy's hair brush, brush, brush'.

Ready for more?

☝ Cover the dolls in chalk, and scrub each part of the doll clean, using body part words.
☝ Practice body part words, such as 'Let's wash dolly's hands/knees/toes, and so on.

Individual needs

- ☼ Make sure the dolls are easy for children with particularly small hands or fine motor difficulties to handle.
- ☼ Encourage children at an early stage of developmen to copy giving dolly a hug.
- ☼ Make sure the dolls and resources used reflect the communities and experiences of the children.

Tiny Tip

✻ Think about the prompts and clues you give to children. Talk to colleagues about their use.

Watch, listen, reflect

- Listen for two word phrases that describe possession or combine an action word with an object word.
- Think about the purposes for which the child is using language, to show you, to give information, to request, to report.
- Watch to see how the children are developing their simple pretend play.

Working together

Parents could:

* try some simple pretend play with their child
* talk to practitioners about their child's play experiences at home

Practitioners could:

* plan a range of simple pretend play experiences, building on everyday routines and events significant to young children.
* check the home corner, updating and refreshing it, keeping it simple, but ensuring it reflects children's home experiences.

Let's Listen

Listening to learn and learning to listen

What are they learning?

are they
- using simple pretend play?
- describing possession?
- using body part & action words?
- making choices?

this leads to
- * creativity and imagination

Walkers, talkers and pretenders

Aspect:
A Skilful Communicator

Component:
Listening and responding

Tick, tick –
listening

What you need

* wind-up musical toys, or
* noisy kitchen timer or small clock, or
* battery operated cassette player and music tape, set at very low volume

What you do

Work with a small group on this activity.

1. Show the children the sound maker. Pass it around, listen to its sound.
2. Listen to all the other sounds you can hear in the room. Try to use and prompt the children to use describing words as well as action and object words.
3. Hide the sound maker in the room, and then help the children listen for and then hunt for the sound maker.
4. Keep encouraging them to stop and listen – what can they hear?

another idea:

* Give one of the children the task of hiding the sound maker.

Ready for more?

- Play this game in other places, maybe a large hall or outside.
- Give each child a simple wooden beater, and then go around the setting or outside together to make lots of different sounds.

34

Individual needs

☼ Frequent coughs, colds and ear infections may cause young children to have temporary mild hearing loss.

☼ Practice listening with hearing impaired children in a quiet place, with fewer distractions.

☼ Encourage children to listen well by removing unnecessary distractions.

Tiny Tip

❄ Wind up musical cot toys are great for this game, as they play on for some time, giving the children plenty of opportunity to find the sound.

Watch, listen, reflect

👁 Watch to see if all the children have understood the game and located the sound.

👁 Listen to the words and phrases they use to report what is happening.

👁 Think about the way the children in the group are relating to each other.

Working together

Parents could:

* listen together and talk about the different sounds that they can hear when they are travelling, at home or in the shops with child.

* at home, remove background noises, such as the television, sometimes.

Practitioners could:

* be mindful of the noise level in the setting, and try to plan some quieter times as well as other noisy parts of the session.

* give children lots of opportunities to experiment with sounds.

Let's Listen

Listening to learn and learning to listen

What are they learning?

are they
    locating sounds?
    listening for different sounds?
    describing words?
    following simple rules?
this leads to
    * commenting and reporting
    * listening

Listening to learn and learning to listen

Walkers, talkers and pretenders

Aspect:
A Skilful Communicator
Component:
Listening and responding

What now? –
listening and responding

What you need

* a hand puppet
* shoe, key, cup, straw, pretend food, book

What you do

Work with a small group on this activity.

1. Introduce the children to the puppet. Let them say hello, stroke it and shake hands with the puppet.
2. Tell them the puppet keeps doing daft things – 'Look he has put a shoe on his hand!', putting the shoe on the puppets hand. Ask the children what the puppet is doing and where the shoe should go. Prompt action words, reporting what they can see and predicting ahead, such as 'I wonder where he will put the shoe next?'.
3. Play on with the different props, with the puppet sitting on the book, putting the straw in the shoe for a drink, tipping the cup upside down, putting food in the cup, etc.
4. Each time, encourage the children with open questions to report, ask questions and predict ahead.

Ready for more?

🖐 Use a small table and ask the puppet to put the cup under the table, When he gets it wrong, ask the children to help the puppet.
🖐 Use a second puppet to make the activity more complicated.

Individual needs

☼ Introduce puppets one to one to children at an early developmental stage. Let them try on the puppet, see your hand going into and out of the puppet and gently stroke the puppet to say hello.

☼ Some children don't like certain textures or soft toy/puppet faces. Be observant and flexible.

Tiny Tip

✳ Puppets don't need to be expensive or commercially produced. A long woolly sock can easily be transformed into all sorts of puppets.

Watch, listen, reflect

👁 Listen to the range of phrases the children use, the sorts of words, such as object, action, describing words and prepositions.

👁 Think about the purposes each child is using language for.

👁 Look at the ways the children are interacting.

👁 Can they show an awareness of each other's personal space?

Working together

Parents could:

✱ encourage their child's attachment to soft toys, including them in pretend play.

✱ try some finger puppets or hand puppets with nursery rhymes or songs.

Practitioners could:

✱ make puppet play a regular part of story and rhyme times.

✱ make sure a few simple puppets are always available to the children to explore and play with.

Let's Listen

Listening to learn and learning to listen

What are they learning?

are they
   listening?
   attending?
   being alongside
   other children?
   responding?
this leads to
   * confidence in
   speaking
   * listening and
   turn taking

Walkers, talkers and pretenders

Aspect:
A Skilful Communicator

Component:
Listening and responding

Two words together –
listening and selecting

What you need

* a wide cardboard tube
* everyday objects and miniature versions of everyday objects small enough to slide down the tube

What you do

Work with a small group on this activity.

1. Spread the objects out on the floor and take turns with the children to slide the objects down the tube, naming each as it goes.
2. Next gather the objects up and spread them out on the floor again. Ask the first child to find two named objects and then slide them down the tube. See if they can find both without a reminder, allow plenty of time before providing a prompt.
3. Give each child a turn to gather two named objects and then slide them down the tube. Try saying 'Ready steady go' before sliding the objects down the tube.

another idea:
* Try this with small pictures of everyday objects.

Ready for more?

🖐 Try posting natural objects such as twigs, stones, cones, shells and so on down the tube.
🖐 Use a pile of toy cars with the tube. Slide all the red ones down, then the yellow and so on.

Individual needs

☼ Use different prompts and reminders as needed, reducing the prompts as necessary.

☼ Give children plenty of time to feel and explore all the objects first.

☼ Spread the objects on a plain background and work in a good light for children with a visual impairment.

Tiny Tip

✳ Shuttlecock & tennis ball tubes are the ideal size for small hands – try asking for used ones at your local sports centre.

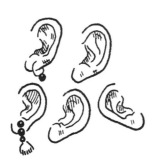

Watch, listen, reflect

👁 Look to see if the children are able to attend to and retain the request for two objects.

👁 Are the children able to maintain their attention when other children are having their turn?

👁 Listen to the words and phrases used by the children. Are they using action words and describing words as well as object labels?

Working together

Parents could:

* save and bring in tubes for this sort of play.
* tell practitioners about the sorts of play their child most enjoys and concentrates on at home.

Practitioners could:

* build listening activities into everyday routines such as washing, snack or meal times.
* add music and story tapes to the book corner, with a very simple children's cassette player.

Let's Listen

Listening to learn and learning to listen

What are they learning?

are they
     understanding two words together?
     listening?
     taking turns?
this leads to
  * sustained attention
  * being part of a small group

39

Listening to learn and learning to listen

Walkers, talkers and pretenders

Aspect:
A Skilful Communicator

Component:
Listening and responding

Surprise! -
what's hiding under there?

What you need

* drawstring bags /old pillowslips
* toy telephone and notepad
* calculator, pencil and paper
* plastic spoon, fork and bowl, shoe and sock
* toothbrush, flannel, pyjamas

What you do

Work with a small group on this activity.

1. Put each group of objects in a pillowslip, or drawstring bag. Pile all the bags on the floor and encourage the children to feel the bags and then each to choose a bag.
2. Take turns to empty a bag. Talk about the objects and what they are used for.
3. Encourage the children to relate the objects to similar ones they have at home, or have seen in other places.
4. Use describing words to talk about colour, shape, size and texture as well as where the object might be kept at home, such as in the kitchen.

another idea:

* Try collections of objects around a theme, such as a visit to the doctors, going shopping.

Ready for more?

* Make this into a simple circle game by passing a bag of objects round, and each feeling and guessing what is inside.
* Place objects on a tray and cover them. Can the children guess by feeling under the towel what is there?

Individual needs

☼ Allow children with sensory difficulties plenty of uninterrupted time and support to explore the objects.

☼ For children needing help with attention difficulties, choose activities that the child most enjoys, perhaps sand play, and bury objects for the child to find.

Tiny Tip

✱ Make a list of key words to model, related to the range of objects you choose for the bags.

Watch, listen, reflect

👁 Listen to the breadth of the children's vocabulary. Are they using any group words, such as 'clothes', or 'food?'

👁 Look to see if they are using pointing and gesture to support their emerging language skills.

👁 Watch to see if children are able to sustain their attention and listen to others and to adults.

Working together

Parents could:

* look for a toy telephone for play at home.
* choose story books with interesting and detailed pictures and play a game of spotting details in pictures.

Practitioners could:

* make sure there are toy telephones in the home corner and that these are modern in style reflecting children's experiences.
* spend a little time every day looking at story books and pictures with small groups.

Let's Listen

Listening to learn and learning to listen

What are they learning?

are they
  using describing words?
  asking questions?
  making comments?
  listening?
  taking turns?
this leads to
  * wider vocabulary
  * confidence in speaking

41

Walkers, talkers and pretenders

Aspect:
A Skilful Communicator
Component:
Listening and responding

42

Stre-e-etch! -
waiting, anticipating, working together

What you need

* squares of stretchy Lycra or knitted fabric
* a large space free of obstacles

What you do

Work with a small group on this activity.
1. Sit with the children holding the edge of the Lycra. Move back until the fabric is spread right out but not stretched.
2. Gradually all lean back slowly stretching the fabric. Chant slowly:
   Pull, pull, pull (pulling the fabric as tight as possible) and
   GO! (releasing the fabric!)
3. Play again, encouraging the children to work together, join in with the chant and release the fabric together.

another idea:
* Put a balloon on the fabric, stretch and release, so the balloon flies in the air when the fabric pings back into place.

Ready for more?

- Try rowing and rocking rhymes with each child working with an adult or with another child, moving together!
- Play 'Follow my leader' games, where the children follow an adult with simple actions.

Individual needs

☼ Make sure the area is free of all obstacles to prevent over excited children getting hurt.

☼ Make sure children with physical difficulties can grip the edge of the fabric.

☼ Try gentle 'To and fro' tugs of war with individual children. This is a great way of developing physical skills.

Tiny Tip

✲ Check out your local market for inexpensive remnants of stretchy fabric.

Watch, listen, reflect

👁 Watch to see if the children are able to time the release of the fabric with the other children.

👁 Think about the range of ways the children are communicating their feelings about this activity.

👁 Listen to the range of words used.

👁 Do the children have the confidence to join in the rhyme?

Working together

Parents could:

* sing and play 'Row the boat' with their child.

* try some bubbles at bath time, encouraging the child to say 'Ready steady go' before blowing and popping the bubbles.

Practitioners could:

* get together and build a repertoire of two-minute games for listening and imitating actions to fill any spare moment in the day.

* talk to parents about how their child's attention and listening skills are developing.

Let's Listen

Listening to learn and learning to listen

What are they learning?

are they
   anticipating?
   listening?
   joining in?
   being part of a group?
this leads to
   * turn taking
   * sharing
   * being part of a group

Listening to learn and learning to listen

Aspect:
A Skilful Communicator

Component:
listening and responding

Resources

toy telephones	real/plastic coins
cups	purses and bags
beakers	paper plates
spoons	garden sticks
plate	feely boxes/bags
clothes	tape recorder
pairs of socks	camera
pairs of gloves	small world sets
small baskets	toy vehicles
dolls	rattles
dolls' clothes	tambourines
cot blankets	shakers and bells

Pictures of people and objects for cards and matching games

Collect some pictures of faces (use catalogues, magazines, old books, brochures, junk mail).

Take some photos of the people in your setting and outside to recognise and name.

Always ask permission before photographing anyone!

Dressing up box checklist

hats	trousers
jewellery	shorts
scarves	swimwear
gloves	large socks
handbags	coats
purses	waistcoat
sunglasses	apron
baby clothes	overall
shoes	briefcase
wellies	saris
slippers	overshirts
ballet shoes	glasses
football boots	cloaks
flippers	skirts
shirts	

Fabrics for dressing up and games

Try **Fabricadabra**! fabric packs from Featherstone Education (01858 881213).

Songs and rhymes

Some action songs

I'm a Little Teapot	Little Peter Rabbit
Five Currant Buns	Here we go round the Mulberry Bush
Miss Polly had a Dolly	There was a Princess Long Ago
Row, row, row your boat	In Cottage in a Wood
The Wheels on the Bus	We can play on the Big Bass Drum
Dingle Dangle Scarecrow	I Went to Visit the Farm one day

Anthologies:

This Little Puffin compiled by Elizabeth Matterson (Puffin)

The Collins Book of Nursery Rhymes, illustrated by Jonathon Langley (Collins)

Bobby Shaftoe, by Sue Nicholls (A&C Black)

Lucy Collins Big Book of Nursery Rhymes, illustrated by Lucy Collins (Macmillan)

Okki Tokki Unga, Action Songs for Children chosen by Harrop, Friend and Gadsby (A&C Black)

The Little Book of Nursery Rhymes compiled by Sally Featherstone (Featherstone Education).

Aspect:
A Skilful Communicator
Component:
listening and responding

The Little Baby Book Series

The structure of the series has been developed to support the Birth to Three Matters Guidance, issued in 2003 by the DfES/Sure Start. The series is structured to follow the aspects contained within the guidance:

Purple Books support the development of a Strong Child:
a child who is secure, confident and aware of him\herself, feeling a valued and important member of their family, their group and their setting.

Pink Books support the development of a Skilful Communicator:
a child who is sociable, good at communicating with adults and other children, listens and communicates with confidence, who enjoys and plays with words in discussion, stories, songs and rhymes.

Green Books support the development of a Competent Learner:
a child who uses play to explore and make sense of their world, creating, imagining, and representing their experiences.

Blue Books support the development of a Healthy Child:
a child who is well nourished and well supported, feels safe and protected, and uses that sense of security to grow, both physically and emotionally, becoming independent and able to make choices in their play and learning.

The First Four books (Published in April 2003) are:
What I Really Want (Purple Books)
I Like You, You Like Me (Pink Books)
Touch it Feel it (Green Books)
Grab and let Go (Blue Books)
The next four books (also containing one book from each aspect) are published in October 2003.

Published in the United Kingdom by
Featherstone Education Ltd
44 - 46 High Street
Husbands Bosworth
Leicestershire
LE17 6LP

47

Would you like to be on our mailing list to receive information about our other products and publications for the under 5s? If so please email your contact details to info@featherstone.uk.com. We will from time to time send you our catalogue and leaflets through the post. We will not telephone you. We will not pass your details to any other company.